DISCOVER MADEIRA

Your Ultimate Insider's Guide through the Wonder's Of Madeira

TONI COLMAN

Copyright © TONI COLMAN, 2024.

All right reserved. No part of this book may be used or reproduced in any manner whatsoever without written permission except in the case of brief quotations enboided in critical articles or reviews.

Table of Contents

CHAPTER 1 5
INTRODUCTION 5
- A Brief Overview of Madeira 5
- Historical and Cultural Significance 6
- Best Time to Visit 8
- Getting to Madeira 9

CHAPTER 2 11
EXPLORING FUNCHAL 11
- Must-See Attractions in Funchal 12
- Shopping and Dining in the City Center 15
- Exploring the Historic Old Town 18
- Cable Car Ride to Monte Palace Tropical Garden ... 20

CHAPTER 3 23
NATURAL WONDERS OF MADEIRA 23
- Hiking Trails and Landscapes 23
- Cabo Girão: Europe's Highest Sea Cliff 26
- Curral das Freiras 27
- Levada Walks: Madeira's Irrigation Channels 29

CHAPTER 4 33
BEACHES AND WATER ACTIVITIES 33
- Porto Santo: A Sandy Paradise 33
- Swimming, Snorkeling, and Diving 35
- Whale and Dolphin Watching 39

CHAPTER 5 43

MADEIRA WINE AND GASTRONOMY 43

   A Taste of Madeira Wine 43

   Local Cuisine and Specialties 46

   Wine Tasting Tours and Experiences 49

CHAPTER 6 53

FESTIVALS AND EVENTS 53

   Madeira Carnival 53

   Festa da Flor: The Flower Festival 56

   Other Local Events and Traditions 58

CHAPTER 7 63

PRACTICAL INFORMATION 63

   Getting Around Madeira 63

   Accommodation Options 66

   Safety Tips and Etiquette 70

APPENDICES 77

   Healthcare, Emergency Services, and Safety tips 82

CHAPTER 1

INTRODUCTION

+++++

Picture yourself on a lush, emerald island rising dramatically from the vast Atlantic Ocean. The air is filled with the sweet scent of exotic flowers and the salty tang of the sea. Welcome to Madeira, a Portuguese paradise that feels worlds away from the bustling mainland of Europe.

As I stepped off the plane for the first time, I was immediately struck by the island's raw beauty. The rugged coastline, framed by towering cliffs and dotted with hidden coves, seemed to whisper promises of adventure. Little did I know that this enchanting island would capture my heart and keep me coming back year after years.

Madeira is more than just a destination; it's an experience that engages all your sensesA. From the moment you arrive, you're enveloped in a world of vibrant colors, intoxicating aromas, and warm hospitality that makes you feel instantly at home.

A Brief Overview of Madeira

Madeira, often referred to as the "Pearl of the Atlantic," is an archipelago consisting of four islands: Madeira, Porto Santo, and the uninhabited Desertas and Selvagens Islands. The main island, Madeira, is where most visitors spend their time, and it's easy to see why.

Spanning just 741 square kilometers (286 square miles), Madeira packs an incredible diversity of landscapes and experiences into its modest size. The island is a natural wonderland, boasting lush laurel forests, dramatic mountain peaks, and sun-drenched coastlines.

One of my favorite aspects of Madeira is its ability to surprise you at every turn. I'll never forget the day I hiked through the island's interior, starting in a misty, prehistoric-looking forest, only to emerge above the clouds to find myself surrounded by alpine-like peaks. It's this juxtaposition of ecosystems and landscapes that makes Madeira truly unique.

The island's capital, Funchal, is a charming blend of old-world charm and modern amenities. Cobblestone streets wind through the historic old town, leading to vibrant markets, elegant gardens, and world-class restaurants. It's the perfect base for exploring the island, offering a taste of city life while never being far from nature's wonders.

Historical and Cultural Significance

Madeira's history is as rich and complex as its famous wine. Discovered by Portuguese sailors in 1419, the island quickly became an important stopover for ships traveling between Europe, Africa, and the Americas.

As I wandered through the narrow streets of Funchal's old town, I ould almost hear the echoes of centuries past. The ornate 15th-century Sé Cathedral stands as a testament to the island's early Portuguese influence, while the colorful street art adorning many buildings speaks to Madeira's modern, creative spirit.

One of the most fascinating aspects of Madeiran culture is its unique blend of Portuguese traditions with influences from around the world. This is perhaps best experienced through the island's cuisine. From the hearty "espetada" (beef skewers) to the exotic "passion fruit pudding," Madeiran dishes reflect the island's history as a crossroads of cultures. The island's most famous export, Madeira wine, has a particularly intriguing history.

Legend has it that the wine's distinctive flavor was discovered by accident when barrels of wine left on ships circling the globe were found to have developed a unique taste due to the heat and movement. Today, a visit to a Madeira wine cellar is like stepping back in time, with some cellars housing barrels that are over a century old.

Cultural events on the island are a feast for the senses. The Flower Festival in spring transforms Funchal into a riot of color and fragrance, while the New Year's Eve fireworks display is said to be one of the largest in the world. I'll never forget standing on a hilltop overlooking Funchal as the clock struck midnight, watching the sky explode with light and color in a truly awe-inspiring spectacle.

Best Time to Visit

One of Madeira's many charms is its year-round mild climate, earning it the nickname "Island of Eternal Spring." However, each season offers a unique experience, and the best time to visit depends on what you're looking for.

Spring (March to May) is my personal favorite time to visit. The island bursts into bloom, with vibrant flowers carpeting the landscape. The famous Flower Festival in May is a spectacular celebration of the island's floral beauty. Temperatures are pleasantly warm, usually ranging from 18°C to 22°C (64°F to 72°F), perfect for hiking and outdoor activities.

Summer (June to August) brings warmer temperatures, typically between 22°C and 26°C (72°F to 79°F). This is the perfect time for beach lovers and water sports enthusiasts. The sea is at its warmest, and the days are long and sunny. However, this is also the busiest tourist season, so book accommodations well in advance.

Autumn (September to November) is a hidden gem of a season. The summer crowds have dispersed, but the weather remains warm and pleasant. This is an ideal time for hiking, as the levadas (Madeira's unique irrigation channels that double as hiking trails) are less crowded. It's also the time of the Madeira Wine Festival, a must-visit for oenophiles.

Winter (December to February) in Madeira is mild compared to much of Europe, with temperatures rarely dropping below 15°C (59°F).

While you might encounter some rainy days, it's a great time to experience the island's lush greenery in full force. The spectacular New Year's Eve celebrations make this a popular time for visitors.

A local tip: If you're flexible with your travel dates, consider visiting during one of Madeira's many festivals. From the Carnival in February to the Atlantic Festival in June, these events offer a unique insight into Madeiran culture and are sure to make your trip unforgettable.

Getting to Madeira

Arriving in Madeira is an adventure in itself. As your plane descends towards Cristiano Ronaldo Madeira International Airport (named after the island's most famous son), you'll be treated to breathtaking views of the coastline and Funchal's amphitheater-like setting.

The airport, once notorious for its short runway, now boasts a modern extension built on stilts over the ocean. It's an engineering marvel that's worth seeing up close. I still remember the thrill of my first landing, the sea seemingly just meters below as we touched down.

Most visitors arrive by air, with direct flights available from many European cities. If you're coming from further afield, you'll likely connect through Lisbon or Porto. Several airlines serve Madeira, including TAP Air Portugal, easyJet, and Ryanair.

For a more leisurely approach, consider arriving by sea. Madeira is a popular stop for cruise ships, and Funchal's harbor is a picturesque entry point to the island. If you're lucky enough to arrive this way, you'll be greeted by the sight of Funchal rising up the mountainside, its white buildings gleaming in the sun.

Once you've arrived, getting around the island is relatively easy. Renting a car gives you the most flexibility to explore at your own pace, but be prepared for some steep, winding roads. If you're not comfortable driving, the island has an excellent bus network, and taxis are readily available.

A word of advice: no matter how you choose to arrive or get around, take a moment to savor that first glimpse of Madeira. Whether it's from the air, the sea, or as you round a bend in the road, that initial view of the island's dramatic landscape is sure to take your breath away.

CHAPTER 2
EXPLORING FUNCHAL

+++++

As the vibrant heart of Madeira, Funchal is a city that seamlessly blends history, culture, and natural beauty. Nestled in a natural amphitheater formed by volcanic hills, this captivating capital greets visitors with a tapestry of terracotta-roofed buildings cascading down to a sparkling blue harbor.

I'll never forget my first morning in Funchal. I woke up early, drawn by the enticing aroma of freshly baked bread wafting through the narrow streets. Following my nose, I found myself in a tiny local bakery, where I savored a warm "bolo do caco" (traditional Madeiran flatbread) smeared with garlic butter. It was a simple moment, but one that perfectly encapsulated the charm of this city – a place where everyday experiences become cherished memories.

Funchal is a city best explored on foot. As you wander its streets, you'll discover a delightful mix of old and new. Historic buildings with intricate balconies stand alongside modern street art, creating a visual feast that tells the story of a city constantly evolving while honoring its past.

Must-See Attractions in Funchal

1. Mercado dos Lavradores (Farmers' Market): This art deco market is a feast for the senses. The ground floor bursts with colorful displays of exotic fruits, vegetables, and flowers. Don't miss the opportunity to taste some of Madeira's unique fruits like the banana passion fruit or custard apple. Upstairs, the fish market offers a glimpse into local life, with fishmongers skillfully preparing the catch of the day.

Expert Tip: Visit early in the morning for the freshest produce and to avoid the crowds. Be cautious of some vendors who may try to overcharge tourists – it's okay to politely decline and move on.

2. Sé Cathedral: This 15th-century cathedral is a testament to Madeira's rich history. Its mix of Gothic and Romanesque styles creates a striking exterior, while the intricate wooden ceiling inside is a masterpiece of Mudéjar artistry. I found the peaceful atmosphere within a welcome respite from the bustling city outside.

3. Santa Clara Convent: This beautifully preserved 16th-century convent offers a glimpse into Madeira's religious history. The simple yet elegant architecture and tranquil gardens provide a stark contrast to the lively streets of Funchal.

4. São Tiago Fortress: This 17th-century fort now houses the Contemporary Art Museum of Madeira. Even if you're not an art enthusiast, the views from the ramparts are worth the visit. I spent a delightful afternoon here, watching boats come and go in the harbor while sipping a glass of Madeira wine at the fort's café.

5. CR7 Museum: For football fans, a visit to the museum dedicated to Madeira's most famous son, Cristiano Ronaldo, is a must. While I'm not a huge football buff myself, I found the rags-to-riches story of this local hero truly inspiring.

Shopping and Dining in the City Center

Funchal's city center is a shopper's paradise, offering everything from local handicrafts to high-end fashion. The main shopping areas are centered around Avenida Arriaga and Rua do Aljube.

For a uniquely Madeiran shopping experience, head to the embroidery shops scattered throughout the city. Madeira's intricate hand embroidery is world-renowned, and these shops offer exquisite tablecloths, napkins, and clothing that make for perfect souvenirs or gifts.

When it comes to dining, Funchal offers a tantalizing array of options that cater to all tastes and budgets. Here are a few of my personal favorites:

1. Restaurante do Forte: Set within the walls of São Tiago Fortress, this restaurant offers stunning views alongside innovative Madeiran cuisine. Their tuna tataki with passion fruit sauce is a delightful fusion of local flavors.

2. O Tasco: For a more casual dining experience, this small tavern in the old town serves some of the best traditional Madeiran dishes I've ever tasted. Their "espetada" (beef skewers) and "bolo do caco" with garlic butter are must-tries.

3. Mercado Velho: This renovated old market building now houses several restaurants and bars. It's a great place to sample a variety of local dishes and wines in a lively atmosphere.

Expert Tip: Many restaurants offer "espada com banana" (scabbard fish with banana) as a local specialty. While it might sound unusual, the combination of savory fish and sweet banana is surprisingly delicious and quintessentially Madeiran.

Exploring the Historic Old Town

The Zona Velha, or Old Town, is the beating heart of Funchal. Its narrow, cobblestone streets are lined with beautifully restored buildings, many of which date back to the 15th century. This area has undergone a remarkable transformation in recent years, evolving from a somewhat neglected part of the city to a vibrant hub of art, culture, and nightlife.

One of the most striking features of the Old Town is the "Arte de Portas Abertas" (Art of Open Doors) project. Local artists have transformed many of the old wooden doors on Rua de Santa Maria into stunning works of art. Wandering down this street feels like exploring an open-air gallery, with each door telling its own unique story.

For a truly immersive experience, I recommend joining one of the guided walking tours of the Old Town. These tours often include visits to hidden gems like the tiny Capela do Corpo Santo, a 15th-century chapel dedicated to fishermen, which you might easily miss on your own.

As night falls, the Old Town comes alive with a different energy. The streets are lined with outdoor seating from numerous bars and restaurants, creating a lively and convivial atmosphere. For a memorable evening, start with a cocktail at one of the rooftop bars overlooking the harbor, then make your way down to the Old Town for dinner and live music.

Expert Tip: Look out for "poncha" bars in the Old Town. Poncha is a traditional Madeiran drink made with rum, honey, and lemon juice. It's potent but delicious, and there's no better place to try it than in a local bar surrounded by Madeirans.

Cable Car Ride to Monte Palace Tropical Garden

No visit to Funchal is complete without taking the cable car ride to Monte. As you ascend from the Old Town to the hilltop suburb of Monte, you're treated to breathtaking panoramic views of Funchal Bay and the surrounding mountains.

The journey itself is an experience to savor. As you glide silently above the city, you'll see Funchal from a whole new perspective. The patchwork of red-tiled roofs gives way to lush green hillsides, and on a clear day, you can see for miles out to sea.

Once you reach Monte, the star attraction is the Monte Palace Tropical Garden. This stunning botanical garden is a testament to the incredible diversity of plant life that thrives in Madeira's mild climate. As you wander through the garden's winding paths, you'll encounter an astonishing array of exotic plants from around the world, interspersed with ornamental lakes, Asian-inspired pagodas, and a fascinating collection of minerals and gems.

One of my favorite spots in the garden is the central lake, where vibrant koi carp swim lazily beneath the surface. I spent a peaceful hour here, sitting on a bench beneath a flowering jacaranda tree, simply soaking in the beauty and tranquility of the surroundings.

For history and art enthusiasts, the Monte Palace Museum houses an impressive collection of sculptures and artifacts, including a remarkable exhibition of Zimbabwean sculpture.

Expert Tip: While the cable car ride up to Monte is undoubtedly scenic, consider taking a different route down. The famous Monte toboggan rides offer a uniquely thrilling way to descend back into Funchal. These wicker sleds, steered by two carreiros in traditional white uniforms and straw hats, have been a tradition in Madeira since the 19th century. It's a heart-pumping ride that offers yet another unforgettable Madeiran experience.

As you explore Funchal, from its historic streets to its hilltop gardens, you'll quickly understand why this capital city captures the hearts of so many visitors. It's a place where history and modernity coexist in perfect harmony, where every turning reveals a new delight, and where the warmth of the Madeiran people shines as brightly as the sun-drenched streets. Whether you're sipping a bica (espresso) in a quaint café, admiring the view from Monte, or simply strolling through the Old Town at sunset, Funchal offers countless moments of joy and discovery that will stay with you long after you've left its shores.

CHAPTER 3

NATURAL WONDERS OF MADEIRA

+++++

Madeira is a natural paradise, an island where Mother Nature seems to have unleashed her full creative prowess. From mist-shrouded mountains to dramatic sea cliffs, from lush laurel forests to otherworldly plateaus, Madeira's landscapes are as diverse as they are breathtaking. As someone who has explored many corners of this enchanting island, I can attest that its natural wonders have the power to leave you speechless, fill you with awe, and reconnect you with the raw beauty of our planet.

Hiking Trails and Landscapes

Madeira is a hiker's dream, offering an incredible variety of trails that cater to all levels of experience and fitness. The island's compact size belies its topographical diversity – in a single day, you can trek through prehistoric forests, scale mountain peaks, and descend into deep valleys.

One of my most memorable hikes in Madeira was the trail to Pico Ruivo, the island's highest peak. Setting out before dawn, I watched the sunrise paint the clouds below in hues of pink and gold. As I ascended through different microclimates, the landscape transformed around me – from hardy mountain vegetation to ethereal cloud forests. Reaching the summit at 1,862 meters (6,109 feet), I felt on top of the world, with panoramic views stretching across the entire island.

For those seeking a less strenuous but equally rewarding experience, the Vereda do Areeiro trail offers spectacular views of Madeira's central mountain range. This trail connects Pico do Areeiro, the island's third-highest peak, with Pico Ruivo. The path winds along narrow ridges and through tunnels carved into the rock, offering breathtaking vistas at every turn.

Expert Tip: Madeira's weather can be unpredictable, especially in the mountains. Always check the forecast before setting out, and be prepared for sudden changes. Pack layers, plenty of water, and sturdy hiking boots. Consider hiring a local guide for more challenging hikes – they can provide valuable insights about the flora, fauna, and geology of the island.

Another landscape that left an indelible impression on me was the Fanal Forest in the northwest of the island. Part of the Laurissilva Forest, a UNESCO World Heritage site, Fanal is known for its ancient laurel trees, some over 500 years old. On misty days, which are frequent, the gnarled, moss-covered trees emerge from the fog like silent sentinels, creating an atmosphere that's both eerie and enchanting. It's a photographer's paradise and a place that feels like it's straight out of a fairy tale.

For a completely different landscape, head to the eastern tip of Madeira to Ponta de São Lourenço. This stark, windswept peninsula offers a striking contrast to the island's lush interior. The barren, rust-colored cliffs and volcanic formations create an almost Martian landscape. The hike along the peninsula rewards you with stunning views of the Atlantic on both sides and, on a clear day, views of the neighboring Porto Santo Island.

Cabo Girão: Europe's Highest Sea Cliff

Standing atop Cabo Girão, Europe's highest sea cliff, is an experience that quite literally takes your breath away. At 580 meters (1,903 feet) above sea level, this vertigo-inducing cliff offers unparalleled views of Madeira's southern coastline, with Funchal visible in the distance.

My first visit to Cabo Girão is etched in my memory. As I stepped onto the glass-floored skywalk that extends over the cliff edge, my heart raced. But as I gazed down at the patchwork of tiny cultivated fields at the base of the cliff and out to the vast expanse of the Atlantic, any fear was replaced by sheer awe at the raw power and beauty of nature.

What many visitors don't realize is that those small fields at the base of the cliff, known as "fajãs," are still cultivated today. Farmers access them by boat or via a recently installed cable car. It's a testament to the resourcefulness and determination of the Madeiran people, making use of every bit of arable land, no matter how difficult to reach.

Expert Tip: Visit Cabo Girão late in the afternoon to witness a spectacular sunset. The way the fading light plays on the ocean and casts long shadows across the cliff face is truly magical. However, be prepared for crowds at this time – it's a popular spot for both tourists and locals.

For the adventurous, Cabo Girão also offers one of the highest cable car rides in Europe. This thrilling descent takes you from the top of the cliff to the fajãs below, offering a unique perspective on the sheer scale of the cliff face. It's not for the faint-hearted, but it's an unforgettable experience for those who dare.

Curral das Freiras

Nestled in a deep valley surrounded by towering mountain peaks, Curral das Freiras (Valley of the Nuns) is a place that seems frozen in time. The village's dramatic setting alone is worth the visit, but its history adds another layer of intrigue to its appeal.

Legend has it that during pirate raids in the 16th century, nuns from a convent in Funchal fled to this remote valley with their treasure, giving the village its name. While the veracity of this tale is debated, there's no denying the sense of isolation and sanctuary that pervades this place.

My first glimpse of Curral das Freiras came from the Eira do Serrado viewpoint, high above the village. The vista from here is nothing short of spectacular – the village looks tiny, dwarfed by the encircling mountains. It's a view that gives you a true appreciation for the village's unique geography and its historical role as a refuge.

Descending into the village itself, I was struck by its peaceful atmosphere and the warm welcome of its residents. Despite its growing popularity with tourists, Curral das Freiras retains a authentic charm. The village is famous for its chestnuts, and if you visit in November during the Chestnut Festival, you'll find the air filled with the enticing aroma of roasting chestnuts and the sounds of traditional music.

Expert Tip: Don't leave Curral das Freiras without trying some local specialties. The chestnut soup is delicious, and the "ginja" (cherry liqueur) served in chocolate cups is a perfect treat after a hike. For the best views, take the cable car from the village center to Eira do Serrado – the journey offers stunning 360-degree views of the valley.

Levada Walks: Madeira's Irrigation Channels

No discussion of Madeira's natural wonders would be complete without mentioning the levadas. These ingenious irrigation channels, some dating back to the 16th century, form a network of over 2,000 kilometers across the island. Originally built to distribute water from the rainy north to the drier south, they now double as one of the most unique hiking systems in the world.

My first levada walk was a revelation. I chose the Levada do Caldeirão Verde, a moderate 6.5 km trail that winds through the heart of the Laurissilva Forest. As I walked alongside the gently flowing water, I was struck by the incredible engineering feat these channels represent. Cut into the sides of mountains, crossing deep valleys, and tunneling through solid rock, the levadas are a testament to human ingenuity and determination.

The beauty of levada walks lies in their accessibility and diversity. Whether you're a seasoned hiker or a casual walker, there's a levada trail for you. Some of my favorites include:

1. Levada das 25 Fontes: This popular trail leads to a beautiful waterfall fed by 25 springs. The sight of water cascading down moss-covered rocks into a crystal-clear pool is truly magical.

2. Levada do Rei: Known as the "King's Levada," this trail takes you through some of the most pristine parts of the Laurissilva Forest. The feeling of walking through this ancient, UNESCO-protected forest is indescribable – it's like stepping back in time to a prehistoric era.

3. Levada do Furado: This levada offers a perfect mix of forest trails and open vistas. The section between Ribeiro Frio and Portela offers breathtaking views of the Machico valley.

Expert Tip: While levada walks are generally less challenging than mountain hikes, some can be narrow with steep drop-offs. Always check the difficulty level before setting out, and consider hiring a guide for more challenging routes. They can provide valuable information about the flora and fauna you'll encounter, as well as the history and importance of the levada system.

One of the joys of levada walking is the opportunity to encounter Madeira's unique flora and fauna up close. Keep an eye out for the Madeiran firecrest, a tiny bird found nowhere else in the world, or the Madeiran orchid, one of the rarest orchids in Europe. If you're lucky, you might even spot a Trocaz pigeon, a species endemic to the Laurissilva Forest.

As you explore Madeira's natural wonders, from its soaring peaks to its deep valleys, from its dramatic sea cliffs to its serene levada walks, you'll understand why this island has captivated nature lovers for centuries. Each landscape tells a story – of volcanic creation, of human ingenuity, of nature's resilience. Whether you're standing atop Cabo Girão, wandering through the misty Fanal Forest, or following a levada through the heart of the island, you're not just observing nature – you're immersing yourself in it, becoming part of Madeira's ongoing natural story.

The diversity of Madeira's landscapes means that no two days of exploration are ever the same. One day you might be scaling peaks above the clouds, the next walking alongside ancient irrigation channels through lush forests. It's this variety, this constant sense of discovery, that makes Madeira a paradise for nature lovers and adventure seekers alike.

As you plan your explorations of Madeira's natural wonders, remember to tread lightly. Many of these areas are protected for good reason, home to unique and sometimes fragile ecosystems. By respecting the environment, staying on marked trails, and taking only memories (and maybe a few photos), you'll help ensure that these natural wonders remain for future generations to enjoy.

In Madeira, nature isn't just something you observe – it's something you experience with all your senses. The feel of the mountain breeze on your face as you stand atop Pico Ruivo, the sound of water trickling along a centuries-old levada, the scent of wild fennel and eucalyptus on the breeze, the taste of sweet chestnuts in Curral das Freiras, the sight of the sun setting behind the cliffs at Cabo Girão – these are the experiences that will stay with you long after you've left the island's shores.

So lace up your hiking boots, fill your water bottle, and set out to discover the natural wonders of Madeira. Whether you're seeking adventure, tranquility, or simply a deeper connection with the natural world, Madeira's landscapes have something truly special to offer. Each trail, each viewpoint, each hidden corner of this island paradise holds the potential for wonder and discovery. The only question is: which natural wonder will you explore first?

CHAPTER 4
BEACHES AND WATER ACTIVITIES

+++++

While Madeira is renowned for its lush landscapes and dramatic cliffs, it's also a paradise for beach lovers and water enthusiasts. The island's volcanic origins have shaped its coastline into a mesmerizing tapestry of pebble beaches, natural lava pools, and crystal-clear waters. Whether you're seeking tranquil sunbathing spots, thrilling water sports, or underwater adventures, Madeira's shores offer a wealth of experiences that will make your island getaway unforgettable.

Porto Santo: A Sandy Paradise

Just a short ferry ride or a quick flight from Madeira lies its sister island, Porto Santo – a hidden gem that boasts one of the most beautiful beaches in Europe. My first visit to Porto Santo was a revelation. As I stepped off the ferry, I was immediately struck by the contrast with Madeira's lush green landscapes. Porto Santo is more arid, with golden hills rolling down to meet a seemingly endless stretch of soft, golden sand.

The beach of Porto Santo is truly the island's crown jewel. Stretching for nine kilometers along the southern coast, this expansive sandy shore is a far cry from Madeira's pebbly beaches. The sand here isn't just beautiful – it's said to have therapeutic properties due to its rich mineral content. I'll never forget the feeling of sinking my toes into the warm, fine sand and watching the turquoise waters of the Atlantic lapping gently at the shore.

One of the joys of Porto Santo's beach is its sheer size – even in peak season, it never feels crowded. You can always find a quiet spot to lay your towel and soak up the sun. The water is calm and shallow, making it perfect for families with children or those who prefer a relaxed swim. For the more active beachgoers, Porto Santo offers a range of water sports. From windsurfing and kitesurfing to stand-up paddleboarding and kayaking, there's no shortage of ways to enjoy the crystal-clear waters.

Expert Tip: Consider spending at least one night on Porto Santo if your schedule allows. The island has a completely different vibe from Madeira – more laid-back and tranquil. Watching the sunset from the beach, with the golden sand stretching as far as the eye can see, is an experience not to be missed. If you're short on time, day trips are available from Madeira, but be prepared for an early start and a full day of travel.

While the beach is undoubtedly the main attraction, Porto Santo has other charms worth exploring. The island's interior offers great hiking and cycling opportunities, with trails leading to viewpoints that offer panoramic vistas of the island and the surrounding ocean. Don't miss a visit to Pico do Facho, the highest point on the island, for breathtaking views.

Swimming, Snorkeling, and Diving

Back on the main island of Madeira, while sandy beaches may be scarce, the island more than makes up for it with its unique swimming spots and rich marine life. One of my favorite aspects of Madeira is how the island has ingeniously adapted to its rocky coastline, creating some of the most unique swimming experiences I've ever encountered.

The natural lava pools of Porto Moniz, located on the northwestern tip of the island, are a must-visit for any water enthusiast. These natural swimming pools, formed by volcanic lava, are filled with crystal-clear seawater that's refreshed with each tide. Swimming in these pools, with waves crashing against the volcanic rocks just meters away, is an exhilarating experience that combines the safety of a pool with the thrill of the open ocean.

For a more secluded swimming experience, seek out the natural pools at Seixal. These lesser-known pools offer a quieter alternative to Porto Moniz, with equally stunning views of the rugged coastline and the towering cliffs that Madeira is famous for.

If you prefer sandy beaches, head to Praia da Calheta on the southwest coast. This man-made beach features golden sand imported from Morocco and calm, sheltered waters perfect for swimming and water sports. It's a great spot for families or those who prefer a more traditional beach experience.

For snorkeling enthusiasts, Madeira offers some fantastic spots to explore the underwater world. One of my favorite snorkeling experiences was at Garajau Marine Reserve, just east of Funchal. The clear waters and abundant marine life make it a snorkeler's paradise. I was amazed by the variety of fish I saw, from colorful parrotfish to graceful sea breams. If you're lucky, you might even spot a loggerhead turtle!

Expert Tip: For the best snorkeling experience, visit in the summer months when the water is warmest and visibility is at its best. Always check the sea conditions before entering the water, as currents can be strong in some areas. Consider joining a guided snorkeling tour – local guides know the best spots and can provide valuable information about the marine life you'll encounter.

For those looking to dive deeper, Madeira offers some world-class scuba diving opportunities. The waters around the island are home to a diverse array of marine life, from colorful nudibranchs to large pelagic fish. Some of the most popular dive sites include:

1. Baixa das Molas: This site features a series of underwater arches and caves teeming with marine life. The play of light through the arches creates a magical underwater landscape.

2. Pestana Reef: Located just off the coast of Funchal, this artificial reef created from sunken boats and concrete structures has become a thriving ecosystem.

3. Ponta de São Lourenço: The clear waters and diverse marine life around this peninsula make it a favorite among divers. Keep an eye out for large schools of fish and, if you're lucky, manta rays.

Whether you're a seasoned diver or looking to try scuba for the first time, Madeira has options for all levels. Many dive centers in Funchal and around the island offer courses for beginners as well as guided dives for certified divers.

Whale and Dolphin Watching

One of the most magical experiences you can have in Madeira is encountering the diverse marine mammals that call these waters home. The seas around Madeira are a haven for whales and dolphins, with over 20 species regularly spotted in these waters.

I'll never forget my first whale watching trip in Madeira. As our boat left the harbor of Funchal, the anticipation was palpable. We hadn't been at sea for more than 20 minutes when the cry went up – "Dolphins!" A pod of Atlantic spotted dolphins was playing in the waves near our boat, leaping and spinning in a joyful aquatic dance. Their grace and playfulness were mesmerizing, and I found myself grinning from ear to ear.

But the real highlight came later in the trip. As we sailed further out to sea, we spotted a tell-tale spout of water in the distance. As we drew closer, I saw my first sperm whale. These magnificent creatures can dive to incredible depths and stay underwater for over an hour, so seeing one at the surface is a rare treat. Watching this giant of the ocean gracefully dive, its tail flukes rising majestically before slipping beneath the waves, was a moment I'll treasure forever.

While dolphin sightings are common year-round, different whale species visit Madeira's waters at different times of the year. Here's a quick guide to what you might see and when:

- **Year-round:** Short-finned pilot whales, sperm whales, Bryde's whales

- **Spring (March-May):** Fin whales
- **Summer (June-August):** Sei whales, Beaked whales
- **Autumn (September-November):** Humpback whales
- **Winter (December-February):** North Atlantic right whales (rare)

Expert Tip: For the best whale watching experience, choose a company that follows responsible wildlife viewing practices. Look for operators that have marine biologists on board to provide information about the animals and their habitat. Early morning trips often offer calmer seas and better visibility.

Don't forget to bring a camera, but remember that no photo can truly capture the awe of seeing these magnificent creatures in their natural habitat.

For those who want a more immersive experience, some companies offer swimming with dolphins in their natural habitat. While this can be an incredible experience, it's important to choose an operator that prioritizes the welfare of the animals and follows strict guidelines to minimize disturbance to the dolphins.

As you explore Madeira's beaches and engage in water activities, you'll discover that the island offers a unique blend of experiences that you won't find anywhere else. From the golden sands of Porto Santo to the exhilarating natural pools of Porto Moniz, from vibrant underwater worlds to awe-inspiring whale watching adventures, Madeira's waters hold endless possibilities for relaxation and excitement.

Remember, the ocean around Madeira is not just a playground it's a vital ecosystem that needs our respect and protection. Always follow local guidelines, respect marine life, and do your part to keep the beaches and waters clean. By being a responsible visitor, you'll help ensure that Madeira's marine wonders remain for future generations to enjoy.

Whether you're lounging on the beach in Porto Santo, snorkeling in crystal-clear waters, diving among colorful fish, or watching a whale breach the surface of the Atlantic, Madeira's aquatic offerings will leave you with memories to last a lifetime. The hardest part might be deciding which experience to try first!

So pack your swimsuit, grab your snorkel, and prepare for aquatic adventures that will take your breath away. Madeira's beaches and waters are calling, promising experiences that will awaken your sense of wonder and connect you with the mesmerizing beauty of the Atlantic Ocean.

CHAPTER 5

MADEIRA WINE AND GASTRONOMY

+++++

Madeira is not just a feast for the eyes; it's a paradise for the palate as well. The island's unique geography, climate, and history have given rise to a culinary tradition that is as rich and diverse as its landscapes. From the world-famous Madeira wine to the hearty local dishes that have sustained islanders for generations, the gastronomy of Madeira is an integral part of the island's cultural identity. As you explore the flavors of Madeira, you'll find that each bite and sip tells a story of this enchanting island.

A Taste of Madeira Wine

No visit to Madeira is complete without sampling its namesake wine. Madeira wine is unlike any other in the world, with a unique production process that dates back centuries. My first encounter with Madeira wine was a revelation – a sip that transported me through time, connecting me to the island's rich history and the generations of winemakers who have perfected this craft.

The story of Madeira wine is as fascinating as its taste. In the 16th and 17th centuries, Madeira was an important port of call for ships traveling to the New World or East Indies. To prevent the wine from spoiling on long sea voyages, producers began fortifying it with grape spirit. They discovered that the constant movement of the ship and exposure to tropical heat actually improved the wine, creating complex flavors that were highly prized.

Today, Madeira wine is still made using a process that mimics these sea voyages. The wine is heated and oxidized in a process called estufagem, which gives Madeira its distinctive flavor profile and incredible longevity. In fact, Madeira is one of the longest-lasting wines in the world – unopened bottles from the 18th century are still drinkable today!

Madeira wine comes in a range of styles, from bone-dry to lusciously sweet. The four noble grape varieties used for Madeira wine are:

1. Sercial: The driest style, with almond notes and high acidity. Perfect as an aperitif.

2. Verdelho: Medium-dry, with smoky notes and a nutty finish.

3. Bual: Medium-sweet, with raisin and caramel notes. Excellent with desserts.

4. Malvasia (also known as Malmsey): The sweetest style, with rich coffee and caramel flavors.

Expert Tip: When tasting Madeira wine, take note of its color – it can range from pale gold for younger wines to deep amber for older vintages. Swirl the wine in your glass and inhale deeply; you'll notice aromas of dried fruits, nuts, and perhaps a hint of caramel or toffee. Take a small sip and let it linger on your palate, appreciating the interplay of sweetness, acidity, and complex flavors that develop with age.

One of my most memorable experiences in Madeira was visiting a traditional wine lodge in Funchal. The cool, dim interior was lined with massive oak casks, some over a century old. The heady aroma of aging wine filled the air as our guide explained the intricate process of making Madeira wine. The tasting that followed was a journey through the island's history and terroir, each wine telling its own story.

For a truly special experience, look for vintage or frasqueira Madeira wines. These are made from a single grape variety and a single harvest year, and must be aged for at least 20 years in cask before bottling. The complexity and depth of flavor in these wines is extraordinary – it's like sipping liquid history.

Local Cuisine and Specialties

Madeira's cuisine is a delightful blend of Portuguese traditions and unique island flavors, shaped by its history and agricultural abundance. The island's fertile soil and varied microclimates allow for the cultivation of a wide range of produce, from tropical fruits to vegetables typically found in more temperate climates.

One of my favorite Madeiran dishes is Espetada, a simple yet delicious meal that epitomizes the island's rustic culinary traditions. Large chunks of beef are rubbed with garlic and salt, skewered on a bay laurel stick, and grilled over an open fire. The first time I tried Espetada was at a local restaurant in the hills above Funchal. The waiter brought the skewer to our table and dramatically slid the succulent meat onto my plate. The beef was tender and flavorful, infused with the subtle aroma of bay leaves and smoke from the grill.

Another must-try dish is Espada com Banana – black scabbard fish with banana. It might sound like an unusual combination, but the delicate flavor of the fish pairs surprisingly well with the sweetness of the banana. The black scabbard fish, with its long, eel-like body and fearsome appearance, is caught in the deep waters off Madeira's coast. Despite its looks, the meat is white, tender, and mild in flavor.

For a taste of Madeira's agricultural bounty, don't miss Bolo do Caco, a traditional flat bread made with sweet potato. It's often served as a starter, slathered with garlic butter. I still dream about the Bolo do Caco I had at a small café in Santana – crispy on the outside, soft and slightly sweet on the inside, with the rich garlic butter melting into every bite.

Expert Tip: For an authentic Madeiran dining experience, look for restaurants away from the main tourist areas. Small, family-run establishments often offer the most genuine local cuisine. Don't be afraid to ask locals for recommendations – Madeirans are proud of their culinary heritage and are usually happy to share their favorite spots.

Madeira's subtropical climate allows for the cultivation of a wide variety of fruits, many of which feature prominently in local desserts. The Passion Fruit Pudding (Pudim de Maracujá) is a delightful end to any meal – creamy, tangy, and not too sweet. For something more unusual, try Bolo de Mel, a dark, spicy honey cake that's traditionally made around Christmas but available year-round.

No discussion of Madeiran cuisine would be complete without mentioning Poncha, the island's traditional alcoholic drink. Made with aguardente de cana (rum made from sugar cane), honey, and fresh lemon juice, Poncha packs a punch but is dangerously easy to drink. My first encounter with Poncha was at a small bar in the fishing village of Câmara de Lobos. The barman mixed it with a carved wooden stick called a caralhinho, explaining that this traditional method helps to blend the flavors perfectly.

Wine Tasting Tours and Experiences

For wine enthusiasts, Madeira offers a wealth of opportunities to delve deeper into its unique viticultural heritage. Wine tasting tours and experiences range from formal tastings at historic wine lodges to more adventurous excursions into the island's wine-growing regions.

One of my most memorable wine experiences in Madeira was a visit to the Old Blandy Wine Lodge in Funchal. Housed in a 17th-century monastery, this historic lodge offers a fascinating glimpse into the island's wine-making traditions. The guided tour took us through dim corridors lined with massive oak casks, some still bearing the names of ships that once carried Madeira wine across the oceans. The tasting that followed was a journey through the different styles of Madeira wine, from crisp Sercial to lusciously sweet Malmsey.

For a more immersive experience, consider taking a tour of the wine regions in the north of the island. I joined a small group tour that took us through the terraced vineyards of São Vicente, where we learned about the unique challenges of growing grapes on Madeira's steep slopes. The highlight was a visit to a small, family-run winery where we tasted young wines straight from the barrel and enjoyed a traditional Madeiran lunch with the winemaker.

Expert Tip: If you're visiting in late August or early September, try to coincide your trip with the Madeira Wine Festival. This annual celebration features grape harvesting experiences, folk dancing, wine tastings, and various cultural events across the island. It's a fantastic way to immerse yourself in Madeira's wine culture and traditions.

For those interested in the historical aspects of Madeira wine, the Madeira Wine Museum in Funchal is a must-visit. Housed in a 17th-century building that was once the residence of American Consul John Burden, the museum offers a comprehensive look at the history and production of Madeira wine. The collection includes antique wine-making equipment, historic documents, and even bottles of Madeira wine dating back to the 18th century.

If you're short on time but still want to experience a range of Madeira wines, many bars and restaurants in Funchal offer wine flights. I particularly enjoyed the tasting at Armazém do Sal, a restaurant housed in an old salt warehouse. Their knowledgeable sommelier guided us through a selection of wines, pairing each with small bites that complemented the flavors perfectly.

For a truly unique experience, some tour companies offer combination tours that blend wine tasting with other activities. I once took a tour that combined a morning levada walk with an afternoon visit to a winery. There's something special about savoring a glass of Madeira wine while looking out over the vineyards where the grapes were grown, with the Atlantic Ocean shimmering in the distance.

As you explore the world of Madeira wine and gastronomy, you'll find that food and drink are much more than mere sustenance here – they're a way of life, a celebration of the island's bounty and cultural heritage. Every meal is an opportunity to connect with the land, the sea, and the generations of Madeirans who have shaped the island's culinary traditions.

Whether you're sipping a rare vintage Madeira in a centuries-old wine lodge, savoring freshly grilled espetada in a mountain-top restaurant, or raising a glass of poncha with locals in a tiny village bar, the flavors of Madeira will linger in your memory long after you've left the island's shores.

So raise your glass and prepare your palate for a culinary adventure. From the complex depths of its world-renowned wines to the simple pleasures of its traditional dishes, Madeira's gastronomy offers a feast for all the senses. Saúde!

CHAPTER 6
FESTIVALS AND EVENTS

+++++

Madeira is an island that knows how to celebrate. Throughout the year, the calendar is dotted with festivals and events that showcase the island's rich culture, deep-rooted traditions, and the joyous spirit of its people. From the riotous fun of Carnival to the breathtaking beauty of the Flower Festival, Madeira's events offer visitors a chance to immerse themselves in the local culture and create memories that will last a lifetime.

Madeira Carnival

Carnival in Madeira is an explosion of color, music, and unbridled joy that transforms the normally tranquil island into a whirlwind of festivity. While Rio de Janeiro might be more famous for its Carnival celebrations, Madeira's version is equally captivating and offers a uniquely Portuguese flavor.

My first experience of Madeira's Carnival is etched in my memory. As I stood on the sidewalk of Avenida Arriaga in Funchal, the anticipation in the air was palpable. Suddenly, the sound of samba drums filled the air, and a wave of color swept down the street. Elaborately costumed dancers moved in perfect synchronization, their feathers and sequins glittering in the sunlight. Behind them came fantastical floats, each one more intricate and imaginative than the last. The energy was infectious – I found myself swaying to the rhythm, caught up in the exuberant spirit of the celebration.

Madeira's Carnival celebrations typically span several days, usually in February or early March (the exact dates vary each year as they're tied to the Christian calendar). The festivities kick off on the Friday before Lent and continue through Shrove Tuesday, known locally as Terça-feira Gorda.

The highlight of the celebration is undoubtedly the grand parade on Saturday night. Known as the Cortejo Alegórico, this spectacular procession features thousands of costumed participants, elaborate floats, and dancing groups from all over the island. The parade winds its way through the streets of Funchal, transforming the city into a sea of color and sound.

But the Saturday parade is just one part of the Carnival experience. On Friday night, the Festa dos Compadres in Santana offers a more traditional take on Carnival. This satirical celebration features large puppets representing various authority figures, poking good-natured fun at local politicians and celebrities.

Expert Tip: For the best views of the main parade, stake out a spot along Avenida Arriaga early. If you want to be closer to the action, consider booking a seat in the grandstands – but do this well in advance as they sell out quickly. Don't forget to bring a camera to capture the spectacular costumes and floats!

One of my favorite Carnival traditions is the "Trapalhão" parade on Shrove Tuesday. This is a more informal, spontaneous event where anyone can participate. I'll never forget the sight of normally reserved bank managers and shopkeepers dressed in outrageous costumes, dancing down the street without a care in the world. It's a reminder that at its heart, Carnival is about letting go of everyday worries and embracing the joy of the moment.

If you're visiting Madeira during Carnival, be prepared to join in the fun. Many hotels and restaurants host Carnival-themed parties, and you'll see people in costume everywhere you go. Don't be shy – this is the perfect time to let your hair down and embrace the festive spirit!

Festa da Flor: The Flower Festival

If Carnival is a riot of color and sound, the Festa da Flor (Flower Festival) is a symphony of scent and beauty. Held annually in spring, usually in May, this festival celebrates Madeira's reputation as the "Island of Flowers" with a series of spectacular events that transform Funchal into a floral paradise.

My first encounter with the Flower Festival left me utterly enchanted. As I walked through the streets of Funchal, the air was heavy with the perfume of thousands of blooms. Intricate flower carpets lined the streets, creating temporary works of art that were as fragile as they were beautiful. Everywhere I looked, there were flowers – in window boxes, hanging from balconies, adorning building facades, and even woven into the hair and clothing of passersby.

The festival begins with the building of a "Wall of Hope" in Praça do Município. Children from local schools each bring a flower to add to the wall, creating a poignant symbol of peace and hope for the future. It's a touching ceremony that speaks to the deep connection Madeirans feel to their island and its natural beauty.

The highlight of the festival is the Grande Cortejo Alegórico (Grand Floral Parade) that takes place on Sunday. Dozens of floats, each one a masterpiece of floral design, parade through the streets of Funchal. Hundreds of costumed dancers accompany the floats, their outfits adorned with fresh flowers that seem to bring mythical creatures and fairy tale characters to life.

Expert Tip: The Flower Festival is one of the busiest times of the year in Madeira. If you plan to visit during this period, book your accommodation well in advance. For the best views of the parade, arrive early to secure a good spot along the route, or consider booking a seat in the grandstands for a more comfortable experience.

One of my favorite aspects of the Flower Festival is the flower market in Praça do Povo. Here, you can find an incredible variety of Madeira's native flowers, from delicate orchids to vibrant bird of paradise flowers. The scent is intoxicating, and it's a wonderful place to pick up some unique souvenirs or simply admire the island's floral bounty.

Throughout the festival, Funchal is adorned with elaborate floral sculptures and displays. I was particularly impressed by the "Gardens on the Square" exhibition in the city center, where landscape architects create stunning temporary gardens that showcase Madeira's diverse plant life.

If you're a photography enthusiast, the Flower Festival offers countless opportunities for stunning shots. From close-ups of intricate floral arrangements to wide-angle views of the colorful parade, you'll find beauty at every turn. Just remember to be respectful of the displays and other visitors as you capture your memories.

Other Local Events and Traditions

While Carnival and the Flower Festival are Madeira's most famous events, the island's calendar is filled with celebrations that offer insight into local culture and traditions. Here are a few that I've had the pleasure of experiencing:

1. Atlantic Festival (June): This month-long event combines a fireworks competition with performances by philharmonic bands and various cultural events. I'll never forget watching the night sky light up with dazzling pyrotechnic displays, each one choreographed to music. The atmosphere in Funchal during these Saturday night shows is electric, with locals and tourists alike gathering to enjoy the spectacle.

2. Madeira Wine Festival (August/September): This celebration of the island's most famous export coincides with the grape harvest. In Funchal, you can witness the traditional grape stomping and enjoy free wine tastings. But for a truly authentic experience, head to the village of Estreito de Câmara de Lobos. Here, I joined locals in picking grapes and even tried my hand (or rather, feet) at traditional grape treading. The festival culminates in a lively parade that pays homage to the island's wine-making traditions.

Expert Tip: If you attend the grape harvest festivities, wear dark-colored clothing. Grape juice stains are considered a badge of honor during the festival, but they might not be so welcome on your favorite white shirt!

3. São João Festival (June): This midsummer celebration honors St. John the Baptist and is particularly lively in Porto Santo. Bonfires are lit, and brave souls leap over the flames for good luck. I was amazed by the carnival-like atmosphere, with music, dancing, and traditional foods like espetada and bolo do caco available at every turn.

4. New Year's Eve Fireworks: Madeira holds the Guinness World Record for the largest fireworks display, and experiencing it firsthand is truly unforgettable. As midnight approached, I found a spot on one of Funchal's hills, overlooking the harbor. When the clock struck twelve, the sky erupted in a symphony of light and color that seemed to engulf the entire island. The display lasted for a full eight minutes, each second more spectacular than the last. It's no wonder that Madeira is considered one of the best places in the world to ring in the New Year.

5. Festa dos Compadres (February): This quirky festival in Santana kicks off the Carnival season with a battle of the sexes. Giant effigies representing men and women trade insults and jokes, poking fun at local events and personalities from the past year. It's a hilarious and uniquely Madeiran tradition that offers insight into local humor and social dynamics.

Expert Tip: *Many of these festivals involve street parades or outdoor gatherings. Madeira's weather is generally mild, but it can be unpredictable. Always carry a light jacket or raincoat, and wear comfortable shoes for standing or walking on uneven surfaces.*

6. Madeira Film Festival (April/May): This annual event celebrates independent film with a focus on nature and the environment. Screenings take place in some of Funchal's most iconic buildings, including the stunning Teatro Municipal Baltazar Dias. As a film enthusiast, I was impressed by the quality and diversity of the selections, as well as the unique venues.

Throughout the year, you'll also find smaller, local festivals in villages across the island. These often celebrate patron saints or local produce (like the Cherry Festival in Câmara de Lobos or the Chestnut Festival in Curral das Freiras). These smaller events offer a more intimate look at Madeiran culture and are well worth seeking out.

Attending a festival or event in Madeira is more than just a spectator experience – it's an opportunity to connect with the heart and soul of the island. Whether you're dancing in the streets during Carnival, marveling at the floral creations of the Flower Festival, or toasting the New Year with a glass of Madeira wine beneath a sky ablaze with fireworks, you're participating in traditions that have been cherished for generations.

These celebrations showcase the warmth, creativity, and joie de vivre of the Madeiran people. They're a time when the island truly comes alive, inviting visitors to shed their inhibitions and immerse themselves in the local culture. From the pulsing rhythms of a samba band to the delicate perfume of a flower parade, from the pop of a champagne cork on New Year's Eve to the sizzle of espetada at a village feast, Madeira's festivals engage all your senses and create memories that will stay with you long after you've returned home.

So when planning your trip to Madeira, consider timing it to coincide with one of these remarkable events. Not only will you experience the island at its most vibrant and exciting, but you'll also gain a deeper appreciation for the rich cultural tapestry that makes Madeira truly unique. Just remember to book early, bring your sense of adventure, and prepare to be swept away by the festive spirit of this extraordinary island.

CHAPTER 7
PRACTICAL INFORMATION

+++++

Getting Around Madeira

As I stepped off the plane and breathed in the fragrant air of Madeira for the first time, I knew I was in for an adventure. But first, I had to figure out how to navigate this enchanting Portuguese island. Fear not, fellow travelers - I've got you covered with insider tips on getting around Madeira like a pro.

By Bus: The Scenic Route

Madeira's bus system, operated by Horários do Funchal, is a marvel of engineering and a testament to the drivers' skills. Picture this: winding mountain roads, hairpin turns, and buses that seem to defy gravity as they navigate impossibly narrow streets. It's not just transportation; it's an adrenaline-pumping adventure!

Expert Tip: Purchase a Giro Card from any ticket office or kiosk. This reloadable card saves you money and the hassle of fumbling for exact change. Plus, it makes you feel like a local!

My favorite bus journey? The number 113 from Funchal to Curral das Freiras (the Valley of the Nuns). As we climbed higher into the mountains, each turn revealed breathtaking vistas of lush valleys and rugged peaks. Just remember to hold on tight - those turns can be sharp!

Rental Cars: Freedom on Four Wheels

For those who crave independence (and a bit of a driving challenge), renting a car in Madeira is the way to go. I'll never forget my first time navigating the island's famous levada roads - narrow paths alongside ancient irrigation channels that offer unparalleled access to Madeira's natural beauty.

Expert Advice: Opt for a compact car with good power. Those mountain roads are no joke, and you'll appreciate the extra oomph when climbing steep inclines. Also, brush up on your manual driving skills - automatic cars are less common and often more expensive.

Cable Cars

For a truly unforgettable experience, take a ride on the Funchal Cable Car. As you glide silently above the terracotta roofs of the old town, the sparkling Atlantic stretches out before you. It's a perfect way to orient yourself and get a sense of Madeira's dramatic landscape.

Insider Tip: Time your cable car ride for sunset. The golden light washing over Funchal Bay is nothing short of magical. Just be sure to bring a light jacket - it can get breezy up there!

Walking: The Slow Travel Option

Madeira is a hiker's paradise, and sometimes the best way to get around is on your own two feet. The island's famous levada walks offer a unique way to explore the lush interior. I'll never forget stumbling upon a hidden waterfall during a levada walk near Ribeiro Frio - the mist on my face and the thundering water created a moment of pure, natural bliss.

Safety Note: While levada walks are generally well-maintained, some can be challenging. Always check the difficulty level, wear appropriate footwear, and bring plenty of water.

Accommodation Options

From luxurious resorts to charming guesthouses, Madeira offers a range of accommodation to suit every taste and budget. Let me guide you through some options that will make your stay truly memorable.

Quintas: A Taste of Old Madeira

For a truly authentic experience, consider staying in a quinta - a traditional Madeiran manor house converted into a boutique hotel. I had the pleasure of spending a few nights at Quinta da Casa Branca in Funchal, and it felt like stepping back in time.

Picture waking up in a four-poster bed, throwing open the shutters to reveal a garden bursting with tropical flowers, and enjoying a breakfast of fresh passion fruit and locally made bolo do caco (traditional Madeiran bread) on a sun-drenched terrace. It's the kind of experience that lingers in your memory long after you've returned home.

Expert Recommendation: Book a quinta outside of Funchal for a more rural experience. The peace and tranquility of the countryside, combined with the warm hospitality of your hosts, will give you a deeper appreciation for Madeiran culture.

Seaside Resorts: Luxury by the Ocean

If you're looking for a bit of pampering, Madeira's seaside resorts offer world-class amenities with stunning ocean views. I spent a blissful week at the Vidamar Resort in Funchal, where the infinity pool seemed to merge with the Atlantic horizon.

Insider Tip: Many resorts offer half-board options. While it might seem pricier upfront, it can actually save you money and allows you to indulge in gourmet meals featuring local specialties like espada (black scabbardfish) and bolo de mel (honey cake).

Rural Tourism: Off the Beaten Path

For a more intimate experience, consider staying at one of Madeira's rural tourism properties. These renovated farmhouses and cottages offer a glimpse into traditional island life. During my stay at a small property in Santana, I woke each morning to the sound of roosters and the smell of freshly baked bread from the local bakery.

Pro Tip: Many rural properties offer cooking classes or guided walks. Take advantage of these to deepen your understanding of Madeiran culture and cuisine.

Budget Options: Hostels and Guesthouses

Traveling on a budget? Madeira has you covered. The island has seen a surge in quality hostels and guesthouses in recent years. I fondly remember my stay at a cozy guesthouse in the heart of Funchal's old town, where the owner's homemade poncha (a traditional Madeiran drink) and stories of island life made for unforgettable evenings.

Money-Saving Tip: Many hostels and guesthouses offer free walking tours or levada walks. It's a great way to meet fellow travelers and explore the island without breaking the bank.

DISCOVER MADEIRA

Safety Tips and Etiquette

Madeira is generally a very safe destination, but as with any travel, it's important to be aware and respectful. Here are some tips to ensure your visit is smooth and enjoyable.

Staying Safe on Levada Walks

Levada walks are a highlight of any trip to Madeira, but they require some caution. I learned this the hard way when I underestimated the difficulty of the Caldeirão Verde levada. Halfway through, the narrow path and sheer drops had my heart racing!

Safety First: Always check the difficulty level of a levada walk before setting out. Wear sturdy shoes with good grip, bring plenty of water and snacks, and don't forget a flashlight for tunnels. If you're not an experienced hiker, consider joining a guided tour.

Respect the Ocean

Madeira's beaches are beautiful, but the Atlantic can be unpredictable. Strong currents and powerful waves are common. During my visit, I witnessed a tourist being rescued after underestimating the power of the surf at Praia Formosa.

Beach Safety: Always heed warning flags and signs. If in doubt, stick to beaches with lifeguards. For a safer swimming experience, try one of Madeira's natural lava pools, like the ones at Porto Moniz.

Cultural Etiquette

Madeirans are known for their warmth and hospitality, but it's important to respect local customs. When visiting churches or entering someone's home, dress modestly. It's also polite to greet people with a friendly "Bom dia" (Good day) or "Boa tarde" (Good afternoon).

Dining Etiquette: In restaurants, it's common for bread and appetizers to be brought to your table automatically. If you don't want these, you can politely decline. Otherwise, you'll be charged for them.

Environmental Responsibility

Madeira's natural beauty is its greatest asset, and it's up to all of us to help preserve it. Always stick to marked trails when hiking, don't pick plants or flowers, and carry out any trash you bring in.

Eco-Friendly Tip: Consider joining a beach clean-up or volunteering with a local conservation group. It's a great way to give back to the island and meet like-minded travelers.

Essential Phrases in Portuguese

While many Madeirans in the tourism industry speak excellent English, learning Portuguese phrases can enhance your experience and show respect for the local culture.

Here's an expanded list of essential phrases, including some Madeira-specific terms:

Greetings and Basics

1. Olá (oh-LA) - Hello

    - Use this as a general greeting any time of day.

2. Bom dia (bom DEE-ah) - Good morning

    - Use until around noon.

3. Boa tarde (BO-ah TAR-de) - Good afternoon

    - Use from noon until sunset.

4. Boa noite (BO-ah NOI-te) - Good evening/night

    - Use after sunset and as a farewell in the evening.

5. Adeus (ah-DE-oosh) - Goodbye

    - A more formal farewell.

6. Tchau (chow) - Bye

    - An informal way to say goodbye, commonly used in Madeira.

7. Até logo (ah-TE LO-go) - See you later

    - A casual farewell, implying you'll see the person again soon.

Politeness

8. Por favor (por fah-VOR) - Please

9. Obrigado/Obrigada (oh-bree-GAH-doo/oh-bree-GAH-dah) - Thank you (male/female)

   - Remember to use "Obrigado" if you're a man and "Obrigada" if you're a woman.

10. De nada (de NA-da) - You're welcome

11. Desculpe (desh-KULL-pe) - Excuse me/Sorry

   - Use this to apologize or to get someone's attention politely.

12. Com licença (com lee-SEN-sa) - Excuse me (when trying to pass)

   - Useful in crowded markets or on busy streets.

Dining and Shopping

13. A conta, por favor (ah CON-ta por fah-VOR) - The bill, please

14. Quanto custa? (KWAN-to KUSH-ta) - How much does it cost?

15. Tem um menu em inglês? (teng oom me-NU eng een-GLESH) - Do you have a menu in English?

16. Saúde! (sah-OO-de) - Cheers! (used when drinking)

17. Bom apetite (bom ah-pe-TEET) - Enjoy your meal

Madeira-Specific Terms

18. Poncha (PON-sha) - A traditional Madeiran alcoholic drink

   - "Posso experimentar a poncha?" (PAW-so ex-pe-ree-men-TAR ah PON-sha) - Can I try the poncha?

19. Levada (le-VA-da) - Madeira's famous irrigation channels and walking paths

   - "Onde começa a levada?" (ON-de co-ME-sa ah le-VA-da) - Where does the levada start?

20. Espetada (esh-pe-TA-da) - A traditional Madeiran meat dish

- "Recomenda a espetada?" (re-co-MEN-da ah esh-pe-TA-da) - Do you recommend the espetada?

21. Bolo do caco (BO-lo do KA-ko) - Traditional Madeiran bread

- "Onde posso comprar bolo do caco?" (ON-de PO-so com-PRAR BO-lo do KA-ko) - Where can I buy bolo do caco?

Useful Questions

22. Fala inglês? (FA-la een-GLESH) - Do you speak English?
23. Onde fica...? (ON-de FEE-ka) - Where is...?
24. Como chego a...? (CO-mo CHE-go a) - How do I get to...?
25. Que horas são? (ke O-ras sow) - What time is it?
26. Pode ajudar-me? (PO-de a-ju-DAR-me) - Can you help me?

Emergency Phrases

27. Socorro! (so-CO-ho) - Help!
28. Preciso de um médico (pre-SEE-zo de um ME-dee-ko) - I need a doctor
29. Onde fica o hospital? (ON-de FEE-ka o os-pee-TAL) - Where is the hospital?
30. Chame a polícia (SHA-me a po-LEE-see-a) - Call the police

Language Learning Tips

- Practice Makes Perfect: Try to use these phrases in real situations. Even if you make mistakes, locals will appreciate your effort.
- Listen Carefully: Madeiran Portuguese has a distinct accent. Pay attention to how locals pronounce words and try to mimic them.

- Learn Numbers: Knowing numbers 1-10 can be incredibly helpful for shopping, understanding prices, and more.

- Use Technology: Download a Portuguese language app or dictionary to your smartphone for quick reference.

- Embrace Mistakes: Don't be afraid to make errors. Most Madeirans are patient and happy to help you learn.

Cultural Note: In Madeira, as in much of Portugal, it's common to greet people when entering small shops or restaurants. A simple "Bom dia" or "Boa tarde" goes a long way in showing respect and courtesy.

Regional Differences: While these phrases will serve you well in Madeira, be aware that some expressions may differ slightly from mainland Portuguese. Embrace these differences as part of your cultural experience!

Remember, language is a gateway to culture. Even if you only master a few phrases, your efforts to speak Portuguese will be appreciated and can lead to richer, more authentic experiences during your stay in Madeira. So don't be shy - practice your Portuguese and watch as doors (and hearts) open up to you on this beautiful island!

As we conclude this practical guide to Madeira, I'm reminded of a moment during my last evening on the island. I was sipping a glass of Madeira wine at a small bar in Funchal, chatting with locals and fellow travelers. The warmth of the people, the beauty of the surroundings, and the rich culture of the island all came together in that perfect moment.

Madeira isn't just a destination; it's an experience that touches your soul. With these practical tips in hand, you're well-equipped to embark on your own Madeiran adventure. From navigating the winding roads to immersing yourself in local culture, every moment on this enchanting island is an opportunity for discovery.

So pack your bags, brush up on your Portuguese, and get ready for an unforgettable journey. Madeira awaits, with its lush landscapes, warm hospitality, and endless opportunities for adventure. Boa viagem! (Have a good trip!)

APPENDICES

Expertly crafted Itinaries

3-Day Whirlwind Tour
Perfect for a long weekend or a short stopover, this itinerary hits Madeira's highlights.

Day 1: Funchal Frenzy
- Morning: Explore Mercado dos Lavradores, sample exotic fruits
- Afternoon: Cable car to Monte Palace Tropical Garden, toboggan ride back
- Evening: Dinner in Zona Velha (Old Town), try the local espetada

Day 2: Natural Wonders
- Morning: Levada walk at Ribeiro Frio (25 Fountains)
- Afternoon: Visit Cabo Girão Skywalk
- Evening: Sunset catamaran trip with dinner

Day 3: Coastal Charms
- Morning: Drive to Porto Moniz, swim in natural lava pools
- Afternoon: Visit São Vicente Caves on the way back
- Evening: Wine tasting at Blandy's Wine Lodge

7-Day Island Immersion
A week gives you time to dive deeper into Madeira's diverse offerings.

Day 1-2: Funchal Focus (Follow 3-day itinerary)
Day 3: Eastern Exploration

- Morning: Hike Ponta de São Lourenço

- Afternoon: Visit Santana, see traditional A-frame houses

- Evening: Dinner in Machico, Madeira's first settlement

Day 4: Western Wonders

- Full day: West tour including Câmara de Lobos, Porto Moniz, São Vicente

Day 5: Mountain Magic

- Morning: Jeep tour to Pico do Arieiro

- Afternoon: Visit Curral das Freiras (Valley of the Nuns)

- Evening: Try poncha in a local bar

Day 6: Beach Day

- Full day trip to Porto Santo island

Day 7: Cultural Immersion

- Morning: Whale watching tour

- Afternoon: Visit Madeira Film Experience and CR7 Museum

- Evening: Fado show with dinner

14-Day Deep Dive

Two weeks allows for a comprehensive exploration of Madeira and Porto Santo.

Week 1: Follow the 7-day itinerary

Week 2:

- Day 8: Funchal food tour, cooking class

- **Day 9:** Golf day or spa day

- **Day 10-11:** Two-day levada trek with overnight stay in mountain hut
- **Day 12-13:** Porto Santo beach retreat
- **Day 14:** Last-minute shopping, farewell dinner at Michelin-starred restaurant

Money-Saving Tips

Transportation
1. Rent a car wisely: Book in advance and compare prices. Consider Madeira's narrow roads when choosing car size.
2. Use public transport: The Horários do Funchal bus network is efficient and affordable.
3. Walk when possible: Funchal's compact center is perfect for exploring on foot.

Accommodation
1. Stay in local guesthouses: Experience authentic Madeiran hospitality at a fraction of hotel prices.
2. Book apartments: For longer stays, apartments can be more economical and offer kitchen facilities.
3. Consider agritourism: Stay on working farms or vineyards for a unique, budget-friendly experience.

Dining
1. Eat where locals eat: Avoid tourist traps; follow locals to find the best value restaurants.

2. Try "menu do dia": Many restaurants offer fixed-price lunch menus that are great value.

3. Shop at markets: Buy fresh produce at Mercado dos Lavradores for picnics.

Activities

1. Free walking tours: Join free tours in Funchal (tip-based) for budget-friendly insights.

2. Hike independently: Many levada walks can be done without a guide; just ensure you're well-prepared.

3. Beach hop: Most of Madeira's beaches and natural pools are free to access.

Sightseeing

1. Invest in Madeira Discount Card: Offers savings on attractions, restaurants, and more.

2. Visit museums on free days: Many museums have free entry on Sundays.

3. Enjoy free viewpoints: Madeira's best views often come free; visit miradouros (viewpoints) around the island.

Shopping

1. Avoid souvenir shops: Buy authentic crafts directly from artisans or at local markets.

2. Duty-free shopping: Take advantage of Madeira's duty-free status for certain goods.

Timing Your Visit

1. Travel in shoulder season: May-June or September-October offer good weather and lower prices.

2. Book in advance: Especially for summer visits or during major festivals.

3. Be flexible: Midweek flights and hotel stays are often cheaper.

Local Experiences

1. Attend free events: Many local festas (festivals) are free to attend.

2. Visit local wineries: Some offer free tastings or budget-friendly tours.

3. Explore public gardens: Funchal has beautiful gardens that are free to visit.

Communication

1. Use Wi-Fi: Many public areas in Funchal offer free Wi-Fi.

2. Get a local SIM: If you need constant connectivity, local SIMs are cheaper than roaming.

Insider Tips

1. Bring a reusable water bottle: Madeira's tap water is safe to drink.

2. Pack smart: Bring layers for mountain excursions and swimwear for spontaneous dips.

3. Learn basic Portuguese: A few words can lead to friendlier service and sometimes better prices.

Remember, the goal is not just to save money, but to enrich your experience. Sometimes, spending a bit more on a unique experience or high-quality local product can be worth it. Balance is key to making the most of your Madeiran adventure without breaking the bank.

By following these itineraries and money-saving tips, you'll be well-equipped to experience the best of Madeira while keeping your budget in check. From the bustling streets of Funchal to the serene heights of the laurel forests, from luxurious wine tastings to simple pleasures like a picnic with a view, Madeira offers unforgettable experiences for every traveler and every budget.

Healthcare, Emergency Services, and Safety tips

Madeira is generally a safe destination with good healthcare facilities. However, as with any travel, it's important to be prepared and informed. This guide provides comprehensive information on healthcare, emergency services, and safety tips to ensure you can enjoy your Madeiran adventure with peace of mind.

Hospitals and Clinics

1. **Hospital Dr. Nélio Mendonça (Main Public Hospital)**
   - Location: Avenida Luís de Camões, 9004-514 Funchal
   - Phone: +351 291 705 600
   - 24/7 emergency services available

2. **Hospital Particular da Madeira (Private Hospital)**
   - Location: Rua do Gorgulho 1, 9004-540 Funchal
   - Phone: +351 291 000 000

- Offers English-speaking staff

3. Centro de Saúde do Bom Jesus (Health Center)

- Location: Rua Nova Pedro José de Ornelas 30, 9060-248 Funchal
- Phone: +351 291 708 180
- For non-emergency medical needs

Pharmacies

Pharmacies (farmácias) are widely available in urban areas. Some stay open late or 24/7 on a rotating basis.

- Look for signs saying "Farmácia de Serviço" for after-hours pharmacies
- Most pharmacies display a list of nearby 24-hour options

Tip: Keep your prescription medications in their original, labeled containers and bring a copy of your prescription.

Medical Insurance

- Ensure your travel insurance covers medical expenses and evacuation
- European Union citizens should bring their European Health Insurance Card (EHIC) for access to state-provided healthcare

Emergency Services

- General Emergency: 112 (works throughout EU)
- Police: 291 208 400
- Fire Department: 291 205 600

- Sea Rescue: 291 213 110

Important: Operators may not speak English. Learn basic Portuguese phrases for emergencies or have a local contact who can translate.

Mountain Rescue

Madeira's mountainous terrain can be challenging. In case of emergency during a hike:

- Call 112
- Provide exact location (GPS coordinates if possible)
- Stay where you are unless instructed otherwise

Safety Tips

1. Crime: Madeira has a low crime rate, but take standard precautions:
   - Be aware of your surroundings, especially in crowded areas
   - Keep valuables secure and out of sight
   - Use hotel safes for passports and extra cash

2. **Road Safety:**
   - Roads can be narrow and winding; drive cautiously
   - Always wear seatbelts
   - Don't drink and drive - laws are strict

3. **Fire Safety:**
   - Madeira's forests can be prone to fires in dry seasons
   - Never leave cigarettes or campfires unattended
   - Report any fires immediately by calling 112

Beach and Water Safety

1. Swimming:
- Obey flag warnings on beaches
- Be cautious of strong currents and underwater rocks
- Natural rock pools can be dangerous during high tide

2. Water Activities:
- Use reputable companies for water sports and boat trips
- Always wear life jackets during water activities
- Inform someone of your plans if engaging in solo water sports

Hiking Safety

1. Preparation:
- Inform your hotel or local contact of your hiking plans
- Carry sufficient water, food, and appropriate gear
- Check weather forecasts - conditions can change rapidly

2. On the Trail:
- Stick to marked paths, especially on levada walks
- Be cautious near levada edges - they can be slippery
- Carry a fully charged mobile phone and a whistle for emergencies

Weather-Related Safety

1. Sun Protection:
- Madeira's UV index can be high; use strong sunscreen

- Wear a hat and sunglasses, especially during midday

2. Heat Exhaustion:

- Stay hydrated, especially during hikes
- Recognize symptoms: dizziness, headache, nausea

3. Rain and Storms:

- Be prepared for sudden weather changes, especially in mountains
- Avoid hiking during severe weather warnings

Health Precautions

Vaccinations

- No specific vaccinations are required for Madeira
- Ensure routine vaccinations are up-to-date (MMR, DPT, etc.)

Food and Water Safety

1. Drinking Water:

- Tap water is generally safe to drink
- In remote areas, stick to bottled water

2. Food Safety:

- Madeira's food hygiene standards are generally high
- Exercise caution with street food and ensure it's freshly prepared

Mosquitoes and Insects

- Mosquito-borne diseases are not a significant concern in Madeira
- Use insect repellent during outdoor activities, especially at dawn and dusk

Altitude Considerations

- Madeira's highest peaks exceed 1,800 meters (5,900 feet)
- If hiking at high altitudes, be aware of altitude sickness symptoms

Traveling with Medications

- Bring sufficient supplies of any prescribed medications
- Carry a doctor's note for controlled substances

Accessibility

- Many hotels and major attractions are wheelchair accessible
- Public transportation may have limited accessibility; check in advance

Solo Travelers

- Madeira is generally safe for solo travelers, including women
- Take standard precautions, especially at night

Emergency Phrases in Portuguese

- "Socorro!" (soh-KOH-roo) - Help!
- "Preciso de um médico" (preh-SEE-zoo deh oom MEH-dee-koo) - I need a doctor
- "Chame uma ambulância" (SHAH-meh oo-mah am-boo-LAN-syah) - Call an ambulance
- "Fui assaltado/a" (fwee ah-sal-TAH-doo/dah) - I've been robbed
- "Onde fica o hospital?" (ON-deh FEE-kah oo os-pee-TAL) - Where is the hospital?

Final Thought

While Madeira is generally a safe destination with good healthcare facilities, being prepared and informed is key to a worry-free trip. Keep this guide handy, stay aware of your surroundings, and don't hesitate to seek help if needed. With these precautions in mind, you're all set to fully enjoy the stunning beauty and rich experiences that Madeira has to offer. Safe travels!

Printed in Great Britain
by Amazon